T0142651

The Luminous Ordinary

Catherine McAuley's Living Presence of Love

Brenda Peddigrew RSM (NL)

The Luminous Ordinary
CATHERINE MCAULEY'S LIVING PRESENCE OF LOVE

Copyright © 2018 Brenda Peddigrew RSM (NL).

All rights reserved. No part of this book may be used or reproduced by any means, graphic, electronic, or mechanical, including photocopying, recording, taping or by any information storage retrieval system without the written permission of the author except in the case of brief quotations embodied in critical articles and reviews.

iUniverse books may be ordered through booksellers or by contacting:

iUniverse
1663 Liberty Drive
Bloomington, IN 47403
www.iuniverse.com
1-800-Authors (1-800-288-4677)

Because of the dynamic nature of the Internet, any web addresses or links contained in this book may have changed since publication and may no longer be valid. The views expressed in this work are solely those of the author and do not necessarily reflect the views of the publisher, and the publisher hereby disclaims any responsibility for them.

Any people depicted in stock imagery provided by Getty Images are models, and such images are being used for illustrative purposes only.
Certain stock imagery © Getty Images.

ISBN: 978-1-5320-5162-3 (sc)
ISBN: 978-1-5320-5163-0 (e)

Library of Congress Control Number: 2018906640

Print information available on the last page.

iUniverse rev. date: 06/07/2018

Special thanks is offered to the Sisters of Mercy of Newfoundland and Labrador, Canada: my teachers, my community, my spiritual sisters, my friends.

…and with very special gratitude to Mary Sullivan RSM
for her diligent collection of Catherine's Letters, called <u>The Correspondance of Catherine McAuley, 1818-1841.</u>
All page numbers in the references are to this book, unless otherwise noted.

as well as

Madeline Duckett, rsm and Catherine Ong, rsm for their booklet called <u>The Mystical Heart of Catherine McAuley.</u>

and to Charlotte Fitzpatrick, RSM (NL), Gabrielle Uhlein OSF, Margo Ritchie CSJ Margie Abbott, RSM(Aus) and Margarita Synnott (Dublin) for diligent proofreading and feedback.

Prologue

I begin this writing on the last day of 2017, after months of daily reading of the letters of Catherine McAuley in the delight of newly discovering her relevant messages to the women who joined her in her beginnings of the sisterhood of Mercy. These words are as relevant today as they were then. Many of the structures that evolved during her time, structures that supported our communities and ministries for two centuries are now beginning to dissolve, which is another word for transformation. So it is heartening to recognize that a thread of Catherine's presence in its most supportive form – personal relationship and consistent encouragement – still leaps and glows from the nearly two hundred plus letters, responses to her letters from others, and sacred documents we are blessed to have, thanks to the early sisters who saved them, and to Mary Sullivan RSM, who gathered and researched and finally published them in 2004.

But where did this begin for me? Turning seventy during the past year raised a special focus: my time in this life now is not unlimited. Somehow, unbidden, this awareness has been rising like a shining thread through my inmost self. One of the expressions of it arose as a pull to visit Ireland one last time (though it may not be the last at all), and that visit deliberately focused on the last two weeks of September, when I could be at Baggot Street for Mercy Day. No other previous visits and work time in Ireland had coincided with that feast before, and it called me.

Not only was I able to spend Mercy Day at the Baggot Street house, but I was invited to read the first reading at the Liturgy, where the chapel was so full that the readers had to sit in the sanctuary for the whole of the Liturgy, which was live-streamed around the world.

Prior to the Mass I spent time sitting at Catherine's tomb, being present and writing. But the surprise came when I went upstairs to sit quietly in Catherine's room for an hour or so. I had done this on previous visits to Baggot Street and always found it a profound and surprising experience. Once, when I was there on retreat several years ago and meditated in her room each morning at 7am, I smelled a strong scent of flowers for two or three mornings in a row, and was shyly hesitant to mention it in the group. When I finally did, the retreat leaders looked at each other and smiled. "Oh yes, Catherine often surprises visitors to that room with her presence," one of them said. That experience stayed with me for a long time and even followed me back to what many call "the wilds of Canada," where I live.

But it was this recent visit that stirred something new and unexpected. Standing before her writing desk, I began to smile and then to laugh, as I realized the literally hundreds of letters that were written at that small desk! I even said – perhaps out loud – "wouldn't you have loved email! You would send out hundreds a day!" Turning from the writing desk, I was caught short by her final words printed in the old fancy style, as follows:

On her death-bed, the last day of her life, being asked to name the sister whom she would like to succeed her, she answered, "The Constitutions give the sisters liberty to choose for themselves and I will not interfere."

*On the same day having desired all the Sisters to be brought to her that she might speak to each as a loving mother, **her first and last injunction to all was to preserve union and peace among each other**; assuring them that if they did they would enjoy great happiness, such as they would wonder where it came from.*
She died on November 11, 1841.

These words stayed with me for the rest of my trip. Some spirit of hers, some luminous thread, lodged in my heart at these words and have pulled me ever since. A few weeks after arriving back home I felt a strong pull to take out once again the collection of her letters and begin to read. Not very far into the reading, morning after morning for about 15-20 minutes or so, I realized the pull, and began to take quotes and notes from her writings for this booklet.

The thread is this, and the above quote contains it: "***her first and last injunction is to preserve union and peace among each other…***"

And so each morning I move through the letters searching for how she herself followed her own injunction, and it is easy to see. She was personal, affectionate to individuals; no detail is too small for her to notice and affirm. And though there are many letters of business and money-worries and all that goes into setting up new foundations – underlining them all – that ***luminous thread of ordinary affection*** is the ground of how Mercy came into being.

It is that thread of relationship that is most important in these times, as some of us begin to face the reality of completion of our present form of living religious life as we have known it. Although the tendency I encounter as I work with many different religious congregations is to emphasize the absolute and primary importance of leadership – I posit a different and more important emphasis: i.e, how we are with one another in community as we face the loss and grief – really the transformation – of our way of life.

As Catherine wrote emphatically at the end of a letter to Sr. Mary de Sales White in Bermondsey, October 18, 1840, at the end of a list of people she asked her to personally greet on her behalf, "Do not forget these little matters."

May all of us, and may some of us even renew our attention to these "little matters," never losing sight of the fact that all our structures grew from that seed of relationship in community.

Catherine's Writing Desk in her Baggot Street Room

1. *A Heart Brimming Over*

"Life's little stories are the building blocks of our journey," says Frank Cunningham, the author of *Vesper Time: The Spiritual Practice of Growing Older.* And so emerge the stories of Catherine McAuley, for her heart was brimming with love – let us not be ashamed of saying it – both for the poor women the sisters served, and for the women who joined her in this service. Catherine's vitality of love literally pours out of her letters. This writing focuses more on the stories of who Catherine was, and is still today, for her particular soul quality is not at all gone from us. As we are called to transforming it into our time, so was she in hers – as we see in the letters – hers was not an easy task, as ours isn't an easy task in these times of diminishment and fulfillment. The amazing miracles of her foundations grew out of just those little stories, and I expect that it is just these very specific, particular examples of her personal, affectionate concern for every sister, old and young, that laid the true foundation stone of the community of the Sisters of Mercy.

One thing became clear to me as I read more and more of her letters. It is this: that Catherine wanted no extraordinary recognition for herself. She was consistently humble and "ordinary" in her presence with the sisters, known for her teasing and joking. It is in the ordinary surprises and demands of every day ordinary life – I learned from her – that light shines through, and not always in the great proclamations of our corporate works.

It is always possible that – in order to highlight a particular characteristic of someone, a distortion of that person can take place. In choosing to follow this theme of Catherine's, I have considered this danger many times, and each time my inner response is that it is not happening in this case. Catherine's loving affection and consistent presence to the sisters, especially individually, is the key to her amazing weaving of the collective wisdom that became the Sisters of Mercy.

More and more often, like Seamus Heaney, in this verse:

> *"And here is love*
> *like a tinsmith's scoop*
> *sunk past its gleam*
> *in the meal bin,"*

a poem in which he sings the praises of the ordinary materials of every day, even what we hardly notice in their important functions, like "the scoop in the meal bin!" I too am filled with the luminous ordinary. Some of these are: the forest which envelops me in deep silence; the animals who live in the forest and in this house; my patient housemate, the work of heating with wood, the daily tasks of shopping and cooking food; the simple, ordinary people around me, and the small exchanges with my own Newfoundland Mercy Congregation as we age and diminish in strength and numbers, buildings and ministries. It is important to note that not all Mercy Congregations in the world are diminishing in numbers, but – like many religious communities, some are. Mine is, and it is out of this context, and my own work with other religious communities coming to completion, that I offer this reflection. At this time, and perhaps more than at any other time, our Luminous Ordinary can shine even brighter. For - at this time in our history, after achievements of monumental proportions beyond Catherine's wildest imagination - it is this *quality of a tender love* that will weave us into the unknown future, and with a thankful peace and faith. For while we must remember – and we must – that Catherine lived in a very particular time, place and culture – the jewels of her soul and spirit are perennial and timeless. And so we receive her multi-dimensional wisdom for our time, which in itself is quickly passing.

In honor of Catherine, and in imitation of her style of rhyming poems, I found myself writing a rhyming poem back to her from this time. Here it is. I hope that – somewhere – she is smiling!

to Catherine McAuley,
inspiration and companion in this writing

It started that day in the house of your dreams_
in that room that was yours – full of grace, so it seems –
all your actual things – teacup and cross,
bedshirt and prie-dieu and all that was lost –
and for me –as if it a personal gift –
your writing desk, source of all that big shift.

I thought of the hundreds of letters it gave you
and how, even now, we all have them to stave off
the sorrows and suffering – a world of deep pain –
no stranger to you, though your letters would gain
a balance in face of it – joys you would share –
humor and laughter and projects to dare.

O Catherine, O Catherine – if you lived in our time,
I wonder if you would still write us in rhyme!
Somehow I think you would do even more
to keep all that darkness away from our door!
All the while praying and planning and dancing,
writing by email and joking and lancing
boils of our troubles and worries and woes –
but wait –
you are here, in the words at our doors.

Your letters, your letters – they brim with your soul,
and I feel all your shining; they make me more bold
to rejoice all through pain and to love without shame,
and how proud I am now to be graced with your name:
MERCY!

2. *Catherine Emerging For Our Time*

Many, though not all, religious communities of women in the Western world are in varying stages of fulfillment, what some call "completion." While this is a situation of denial for some and grief for others, small threads of light are also emerging, illuminating the unfolding of the larger, longer history that this situation announces. Diarmuid O'Murchu's writing in *Religious Life in the 21ˢᵗ Century* presents that long history, concluding with what is happening in our own time, and visioning that reality as it might continue after those of us alive now have passed on. Looking back through history, we can easily see that it has happened many times before. We are in that cycle of unfolding forms.

My consistent experience in reading through all of Catherine's letters, day after winter day of this cold year, was the evident warmth of Catherine's heart, demonstrated so consistently in her daily relationships with the women who joined her. In *Mystical Heart,* she is quoted as saying "How can we teach the love of God if our hearts are cold?"(p.17) It was from the warmth of her own heart that the community grew, and it is to this quality that I return day after day, examining my own heart in relationships on all levels. It is not easy, which makes Catherine all the more luminous in her words and in the difficulties and hardships which she encountered daily. Hers was not an easy time in which to live; neither was her endeavor affirmed and approved from the beginning. Some of her most difficult obstacles arose from the very Church she sought to serve. Even in this, her cheer, humor and laughter prevailed, lifting her sisters into a different realm from all their obvious daily difficulties.

What of her life stands out as being significant for the difficulties of our own living? What of her words reach across time to sustain our own hearts in the difficulties of ours? In a small way, it is my intention to lift out such possibility, such presence. For it is a certain truth that throughout my reading of the letters I felt her presence. I felt an ease, and a kind of joy, which I hope to pass on through this attempt to go into her heart and find the light that awaits us all there.

What qualities of hers shine through that would help us today in the pains of loss and diminishment? I have chosen five that shine through my reading, and these are ones that we can all benefit from in these days of our lives.

Here are the ones we can draw inspiration from as we face our own realities of diminishment and completion:

A. Humor and "Merriness"
B. Warm affection and tender concern for the sisters
C. Everyday spiritual practice
D. Ongoing Sources of Stress and Anxiety
E. Visible/Invisible Presence of the Holy

A. Humor and "Merriness"

Because this quality is so unique to Catherine, especially as a foundress of a religious community of women, I have decided to start with this capacity on her part to lighten serious and dire situations, especially her own, and to relate to her sisters in this way so as to encourage them in stepping out of their own serious tendencies as they too encountered difficult and painful situations. Her humor, often expressed in rhyming poems, a few of which I will include here – though there are too many to include all – not only lightened situations and relationships, but brought laughter; what Catherine often called "merriness." It is important to realize that such humour lightened encounters and relationships that could not always be addressed seriously, though their content and purposes were serious indeed. It is good to also remember the 1830's as being not very amenable to the opinions of women on any subject. In this light, Catherine found through her humour a way to share her very definite opinions and encouragements to the sisters. Even though all her letters have to be perceived as reflecting the times and the culture in which she lived, we can – from our own understanding – also "translate" them into our culture – a time in which high profile women are only now publicizing the controlling abuse many had to suffer in order to move into careers of their own choosing.

If there is one quality that sets Catherine apart, it is this way she had of finding humor in the most dire of situations, including her own health. Once she writes ""I carry my child in its cradle," referring to her broken arm in its sling (p.106) or "I am now going to hide from the doctor" (p. 367) – this when she was in the last stage of her illness – she died soon after that remark.

Sometimes Catherine used humor to mask complaints, as in her acrostic poem to the Reverend Peter Butler in Bermondsey, England, after she had been there visiting the English Foundation; in fact, in this instant she wrote two:

F = For wild Irish did you take us

A= As some English folk would make us

T= Thinking we just ran away – from

H= *Hirish* houses made of clay

E= Ever glad to change our station

R= Rushing to another nation

B= Bermondsey – we'll not forget

U= Under cold and damp and wet

T= Tis true we must all seasons meet

L= Leaving our calm, our loved retreat

E= Engaged in sorrows not our own

R= Refreshed – by all that's neat at home

and the second one to Fr. Butler, written immediately after the first:

F= For pity's sake, Sir, will you cover the Porch

A= As now the wet season draws nigh

T= Too often we've passed by the light of a Torch

H= Heavy rain dripping down from the Sky

E= Every Sister caught cold in the dreary damp Way

R= Repeatedly they'd to pass over

B= Beyond eighteen times in the course of a Day

U= Under rain- without footpath or cover

T= To the young and the old it alike was severe

L= Lungs – teeth-eyes or head felt the smart

E=Each one could say – oh, tho' tis so near

R=Run fast – the cold pierces my heart.

Often, some of her most serious messages were conveyed with humor, as is this one, telling how tired she was when making a walking trip to Dun Laoghaire. In a long, rhyming letter to Sr. Mary Ursula Frayne in mid-1838, she concludes with these verses:

"By hills and by hollows –through great rocks and stones
expecting each moment to break my poor bones
until quite exhausted of temper and strength
I gave up to despair and fell down at full length
on a deep slooping[sloping] rock – from which the least tip –
would – or I thought so – have caused me to slip
At length I got up and did fervently pray
that the good guiding spirit would bring me through that Day
Again we arrived at a steam train house gate
and had not now more than 10 minutes to wait
by our long walk – the rest of the day seemed much shorter
and – we reached our dear convent in time for the quarter.

P.S. All things that you asked for I'm trying to get
But pray ask no more – my own dearest Pet
I'll now take my leave – Be a good child
humble – and merry – diligent and mild
Work hard for the poor, love one another
and believe me your ever affectionate Mother."

There were even poetic exchanges about customary rules, a kind of jousting, as is shown in a back-and -forth exchange with Sister Mary Francis Marmion (p.121-122) regarding permission for the sisters to talk a little more in the run of their day!

And then there is "the lady of flesh and bone", in which Catherine writes "My dear Sister Mary Teresa (Purcell) describes a melancholy night she passed while her mother was so ill. "We must banish all these visionary matters with laughing notes (musical notes drawn on the page) hop-step for the ceremony, to be concluded with "The Lady of Flesh and Bone". We will set up for a week what is called a nonsensical Club. I will be president, you vice-president, and Catherine (herself) can give lectures as professor of folly." (p.76)

In the footnote to this paragraph it is said that "Catherine was known to have a large store of songs, including Dublin street ballads, in her repertoire, many of which she sung at recreation.

'The Lady of Flesh and Bone' was one of these – it was an ancient Irish version…of an old English nursery rhyme…" The part some of us might be familiar with is that old childhood chant "the worms crawled in, the worms crawled out…"

With some of the sisters so inclined, Catherine also carried out poetic exchanges. One of these was Sister Mary Teresa Vincent Potter. The lines quoted below are from a longer exchange between them, in response to an earlier poem or poems, no longer in existence. Some lines indicate that it was written at the turn of the year (early 1839) about a month after Mary Teresa Vincent Potter's reception of the habit in Limerick on December 4, 1838. This poem continues a correspondence in verse that will end only with the death of Catherine's "sweet little poet" on March 20, 1840. (p. 174, 175 of letters):

The 38th year is now past
Its cares and its pleasures are gone
the 39th may be our last
since the last is so surely to come
Let us beg for renewed animation
in discharge of our duties each day
let us smile under every privation
that religion has strewn in our way
All coldness and choler we'll smother
and watchfully shun all dejection
we will cordially love one another
since that is the mark of election.

And indeed, some of the sisters wrote back to her in rhyme, in similar style and for similar purposes. Here is one from Mary Ursula Frayne, written to Catherine from Booterstown (April 30, 1839):

My Dear Reverend Mother, on this Festive Day
Some words in your honor I gladly would say,
But vain the endeavor, in vain do I try –
My muse is too humble for subject so high
Yet tho' *louder* expressions of joy you may hear
I'll answer for it, they are not more sincere
Than that felt by your children who with me unite
In begging the favor about which I write
That you'll send Sister Celia, your 'presentative here
And M. Aloysius, to the sisters so dear
Before dinner today, as it would not be fair
to leave us *here* orphans and keep both Mothers there

A pity it were that a day of such joy
Should bring with it even a shade of alloy
Which must be the case, unless you will please
To grant us this favor, as you can with great ease
If they come in the Train they'll be here in less time
By far than I spend in writing this rhyme
I know you will grant us this favor today
As on reading those lines I expect you will say
"I cannot refuse them so just a request
Then go back, my dear Sisters, I think it is best
Be merry and joyous in B town tonight –
St. Catherine's Day to all bring delight.

Each poem in this collection – and many were lost – surely we know that Catherine never envisioned them being read by any than the intended recipient – is a communication of Catherine McAuley's inmost heart. She was surely – above all, a woman of heart presence, her emphasis on connection, affection and a weave of common purpose fueled by loving regard for each and every one of them, even the ones who sometimes were sources of irritation and misunderstanding. But isn't that real life?

Finally- and I encourage anyone reading this short essay to revisit the Letters again for more poems of many kinds – Catherine's humour is not only expressed in poems, but in the encounters and incidents she chose to tell about in her letters. Here is a paragraph from a letter she wrote to Sr. Mary deSales White from Baggot Street on October 18, 1840, the year before she died:

"Mother de Pa[zzi] and I have kept up the most musical sighing or groaning in the Bishop's Parlour. I thought she was far surpassing me – and yesterday I determined not to be outdone and commenced such a moaning as brought all to an end."

Finally – and in my own tribute to the Presentation Sisters – is this paragraph of one of Catherine's letters to Frances Ward:

"We visited our old George's Hill – they were delighted and so was I,
said I would kiss the chairs and tables – but by some mistake I kissed
a grand new chair in the Parlour! However I managed, as ducky Mary
Quin used – (your mother) – I took it back and brought up the old rush
chair I used to sit on in the novaship!"

What are we to make of such spirit, such humor, such intimate grace, in these times of our own serious issues, of transforming a way of life that Catherine initiated and nurtured and gave her life to? What leadership she offers us even now – the humility, the humor, the foundation of personal affection on which she humbly built her ways of healing and educating women who had so much less?

This section of nonsense/message poems could continue, but there are many more aspects to Catherine's character and personality that are supportive, sustaining, and inspiring. I close this section with a quote from Mary Sullivan's collection of her correspondence:

The most striking feature of this period [beginning November 6, 1840 – her death on November 11, 1841] is Catherine McAuley's fidelity to her duty, as she perceived it, of letter-writing to the "foreign powers" – her playful term for the superiors and other sisters in the foundations outside Dublin. Catherine felt a deep obligation to support and encourage them by way of her affection, her good humor, and a sharing of news when visits were impossible. (p.310)

B. Warm affection and tender concern for the sisters

While Catherine's strong relationships with her sisters were uniquely expressed in humor and the nudge to "merriment" (a word she loved, my conclusion from her frequent use of it), it was also directly expressed in the common language of her letters to them, her frequent, almost daily letters. How little, in comparison, she writes of work, compared to how often she speaks to and of each Sister, personally, profoundly, supportively. Her language and imagery is characterized by this affection, and it appears in every letter except the formal ones to clergy. But to her sisters – even the postulants – these letters are filled with love and affection, expressed directly. And while Catherine did not approve of "particular friendships "in community", (p.247, Footnote 8), her encouragement and example of affection for all is quite a distinctive mark of her own relationships with everyone.

Here are some expressions and affirmations of this affection taken directly from her letters:

"The offering of genuine affection has everything to enhance its value" (letter to Sister Mary Elizabeth Moore, Limerick) p.201.

"Tell my dear Sr. M. Vincent I am quite disappointed that she never writes me one little note." (p. 208)

To a postulant, a mixture of affection and humor: "It has given me great pleasure to find you are so happy, and I really long for the time we are to meet again – please God – but the good Mother Superior will not have equal reason to rejoice, for I am determined not to behave well and you must join me." (pp. 28-29)

"I never for one moment forgot you or ceased to feel the most sincere interest and affection – so forgive all my past neglect…"(p. 262) to Sr. Mary Vincent Hartnett

"accept these few lines, which proceed from my heart, earnestly hoping you are as well and happy as I wish you to be…" (to Sister Mary Josephine Warde, early November, 1837, p.101), and again to her –

"Thanks be to God you are so happy, indeed it affords me real comfort. The contrary would afflict me very much." (January 27, 1838, p. 123)

"I saw Sr. Mary Teresa on Sunday last. She desired a thousand loves to you…" (p. 129)

"I am not fit to appear… perplexed and weary – out of conceit with everything – I sit down to talk to my own dear old companion and affectionate child. Your packet was most joyfully received, and your letter read again and again, as a solace and comfort which God sent me. "(p. 139 to Frances Warde)

So not only did Catherine write and send letters, but she expresses often how important it is to her to receive them, as in the previous quote, and this one:

"My ever dear Sr. Mary Frances…my mind has been uneasy at not writing to you…write to say particularly how you are. [I hear] you have some return of your distressing feelings. I look forward with delight to the day I shall see you once more." (p.159)

And finally, one of her/our most famous Mercy quotes, known by us all:

One thing is remarkable…that no breach of charity ever occurred
amongst us. The sun, I believe, never went down on our anger.
This is our only boast…(p. 180)

I wonder, when I read this now, whether that saying of hers became so familiar that we lost its truth. I wonder whether we have elevated her to the point where we unconsciously lost connection with the reality of her experience and her relationships with the sisters, and whether the words became so familiar that we relegated them to an earlier time and lost that strong message that here is where and how we began, and here is where and how we can – with Catherine's affectionate blessings – embrace our transformation.

C. Everyday Spiritual Practice

More than any other of Catherine's writings, it was her spiritual maxims that were passed down to those of us honored enough to become a part of her Congregation of women. As I intimated earlier, these became familiar – that is – spoken so frequently we could think "this is really who she was" when she was so much more - that she was removed from the fullness of the reality of who she was. Now, placed in the context of her larger life, these spiritual maxims find their deeper place of reality and grace for all of us.

In a powerful booklet by Madeline Duckett rsm and Caroline Ong rsm, called *The Mystical Heart of Catherine McAuley,* the authors summarize their powerful and relevant reflection in these words"

> *Her story is a story of action-contemplation par excellence.*
> *It is a story for a time such as ours, so caught up with action,*
> *busyness and the push to do more and more…she is a living*
> *example of how our hearts, like hers, "can always be in the*
> *same place centred in God." Thank you, Catherine, for what*
> *you share with us if we sit still enough and long enough to*
> *listen to your Mercy wisdom, a wisdom that reaches into the*
> *wells of practical mysticism and takes us to the Source…(p. 53)*

Catherine's spiritual practices remain for us a concrete practice of contemplation and action woven into every day. They tell us of her sorrows as much as her joys; in fact, I suspect that she had so many sorrows that her spiritual practices were strengthened by how much she depended on them for strength.

One of the famous teachings that Catherine repeated in her "Retreat Instructions" is "Each day is a step which we take towards eternity." Catherine's focus on the "each day" – of staying in the present and seeing each day as just as significant as "eternity" echoes current mindfulness and Buddhist teachings. It is a perennial practice of deepening spiritual presence in everyday life, too large to be confined to any one religion. Catherine's multi-dimensional spiritual presence would be well-recognized today.

Some others of her words – all from *The Correspondance of Catherine McAuley*:

- ❖ "Submit we must, but we should do much more. We should praise and bless the hand that wounds us.(p.99)

- ❖ "Put your whole confidence in God." (p. 115)

- ❖ "There we find a nice little cross." (p. 119)

- ❖ (to Teresa White) "I charge you, my dear child, not to be sorrowful – but rather to rejoice if we are to suffer this humiliating trial…I feel it would give you no consolation were I to say 'God would not be displeased with you – though he may be with me –" (p. 164)

- ❖ "Don't let crosses vex or tease/ try to meet all with peace and ease./Notice the faults of every day/ but often in a playful way…" (p.169)

- ❖ "I like the Irish piety better – it seems more genuine – though not nearly so much exteriorly."(p.220)

- ❖ "my darling Sister Mary Elizabeth, I did not think any event in the world could make me feel so much. I have cried heartily – and implored God to comfort you – I know he will." (p.259)

These (very) few examples of Catherine's deep faith and spirituality, lived most realistically in unpredictable and difficult circumstances – many of which will be addressed in the next section of this booklet – offer encouragement and sustenance in the dire realities we face today. The content is different but the faith, the simplicity of faith and trust cannot be unseen. And the love – well- *daily,* she offered so many expressions of love and humor (which made the love possible) – for her sisters, for the poor and the sick, for her family, for the struggling reality of her world – how can we do any less? Surely our world cries out as much as hers? Surely, even in our diminishing physical powers and the shrinking of properties our presence, the fullness of our years can shine even brighter in Catherine's way? Perhaps we yet have something the world needs – just not as we thought it might…

D. Ongoing Sources of Stress and Anxiety

It is very easy, reading what we have so far in this booklet, to believe that Catherine was able to do all that she did easily. We could get the impression that her way of making light of difficulties served to actually lighten the burden for her, which was not always the case. Catherine McAuley suffered greatly, in many ways, and I want to touch briefly on them in this section so that we also know that our own trials and sufferings can find ground and consolation in her presence and her encouragement.

The three most readily identifiable sources of Catherine's stress and anxiety were

a. resistance and criticism from clergy;
b. health – her own and the sisters', including deaths of family and of the sisters themselves.
c. resources sufficient to sustain houses and ministries.

a. Resistance and Criticism from Clergy

Mary Sullivan RSM summarizes best a short introduction to this painful section:

After only six years of its founding the Sisters of Mercy had garnered episcopal approval and support and had been invited to open houses in four other parts of Ireland: Tullamore (1836), Charleville(1836), Carlow (1837) and Cork (1837). But the last months of 1837 were a very painful period in Catherine's life for one specific reason: a deep conflict arose between her and Dr. Walter Meyler, parish priest of St. Andrew's Church, over his unwillingness to assign a regular chaplain to serve the sacramental needs of the homeless women and girls sheltered in the House of Mercy on Baggot Street. This 'unwarranted abuse of Church authority' (to quote Dr. Andrew Fitzgerald) – caused her more anguish than the saintly death in October of the Mary de Chantal McCann, the fifth to die in 1837, or the pain she suffered in November, when she broke her left wrist, severely injuring the sinews, in a fall down stairs while visiting the sisters in Kingstown… but the 'bitterness' she felt at the injustice of the chaplaincy controversy was a new kind of suffering for her; it was assuaged only with prayer, effort on her part, and the support and counsel of her friends." (Mary Sullivan RSM, p.94 in <u>The Correspondance of Catherine McAuley</u>).

Although there were other tripping points with clergy throughout the few short years during which Catherine tirelessly and with unimaginable physical cost to herself "founded" the Sisters of Mercy, nothing affected her as much as this deep wound. In her own words to Sister Mary de Pazzi Delaney, October 3, 1837, she says:

"My dearest Sister Mary, will you please relieve me from the distressing business about the chaplain. It is constantly before me, and makes me dread going home. I know it is not possible for me to have any more argument with Dr. Meyler without extreme agitation…I will never depart from the advice Mr. Armstrong gave me, that I would sooner leave the parish entirely…I am sure the Bishop would not ask me to do what Mr. Armstrong so long and so determinedly objected to……and will you, my dear, speak to Mr. Lynch and say in the most decided manner that we require a chaplain to the house and *cannot nor will not* call on any of the parish clergymen to attend to the institution…*do get me through this – don't be afraid.* Perhaps one third of what I have said will be more than sufficient – and this is the reason I dread the subject – because I find myself impelled to *say too much.*" [Here a sizeable portion of the autograph letter has been cut out.]

The intensity of this controversy is evident in Catherine's unusually strong language and in her attempts to cut off her own impulse to say more. Her suffering – both her own and for the sisters – must have been excruciating at times – so much so that she asked someone else to engage it on her behalf. There are more hints of her interior struggle in this letter quote to Sister Mary Teresa White (October 17, 1837):

"When I promised to go to my dear Sr. Frances in time of trial, you may be sure, my dear child, I did not mean the trial which death occasions, with which I am so familiarized that the tomb never seems closed in my regard. I alluded to those difficulties which her new state exposed her to – such as incurring the displeasure of her spiritual superiors, without intention, or experiencing marks of disapprobation, and *not knowing why.*"

"The Kingstown business is a real portion of the Cross. From what you say, I should think you do not know all the circumstances. They were submitted to the Bishop already…indeed, when I think of what my poor Sisters suffered, I do not wish they should return, though I feel very much for the poor souls they have left." (to Sister Mary de Pazzi Delany, Baggot Street, November 15. 1838)

"I could not describe Mr. Cavanaugh's surprise. He said Mr. Sheridan could not speak plainer. He wrote to him expressing his surprise and shewed me a copy of the letter. If it was to me he said it – he would think it my imagination.

 I think it would seem like defiance – if I were to go now, after the Parish Priest saying to two Sisters, in the presence of his curate, that he never invited them…it is a perplexing business."(p.184-85)

"Did you tell Sr. Mary Aloysius my two reasons for wishing you or she would say something to the vicar as to your visit – first, that he would not regard me as Mistress General." (p. 370)

We know from evidence in her letters that Catherine had other clergy supports and helps for her sisters and her strongly emerging yet fledgling congregation, but it is her pain that comes through here, and in so many letters, which is important for us – her followers – to realize, her conclusion at the end of a letter to Sr. Mary Frances Warde describing her clergy dilemmas as "a perplexing business."(p.185) For only then can Catherine become real for us, among us, as many of us encounter the pain of this time in our history – for many, a time of diminishment, not of flourishing.

b. Health: her own and the sisters'

Unlike our own time in the twenty-first century, health realities in Ireland in the 1800's would be in many cases, primitive and undeveloped. And this we see and hear, through Catherine's letters and laments, of the deaths of young members, and the worse states of those in poverty whose needs the sisters tried to address.

"As to my delay in writing I have been tortured with my unfortunate mouth – only just getting a little better. We are very near a full stop – feet and hands are numerous enough, but the heads are nearly gone."(p.151)

"my sight is getting worse and my fingers stiff…" (p.180)

"Our dear Mother had a miserable time of it…being almost constantly ailing. I always thought that the Bermondsey Foundation was the beginning of her death-sickness, for she was never perfectly well after…"(Mary Teresa White, p.244)

"This is a shameful letter. I am nervous. We will be anxious to hear from you. Your affectionate M.C. McAuley. (to Sr. M. Frances Warde, 10 March, 1840)

"I have just been speaking to Father O'Hanlon of your request – he says he will go himself, but that is very doubtful. It would add fifty miles to my traveling – I who am journeying fast enough out of this world. Every day I am weak at some time. My stomach has never recovered its last attack – frequent swelling and soreness." (Catherine McAuley to Sr. M. Elizabeth Moore, 14 March, 1840)

Through all that filled her life of "founding" the Sisters of Mercy, Catherine was always connected to her own family. One example is sufficient here: "My poor James (nephew) is in the last stage of decline in Kingstown. I am as much there as possible. Pray and get prayers for him."(p.305)

From p. 305 in the letters and onwards, the pages are full of notes about sisters everywhere sick and dying with typhus. As in other places during that time, many young people died, including several members of the new community. Catherine herself was beginning to show signs of fatigue:

"My fingers are so stiff I cannot write anymore." (p.307). With her handwriting seriously deteriorating we hear shortly afterwards of other sisters writing letters at her dictation, including her last will and testament in letter #168.

So important was it that she stay connected to the sisters, that between March 19, 1840 and November 11, 1841 – the day of her death – she wrote 152 letters! As Mary Sullivan writes on p. 310:

The most striking feature of this period is Catherine McAuley's fidelity to her duty, as she perceived it, of letter-writing to "the foreign powers," her playful term for the Superiors and other Sisters in the foundations outside Dublin.

Catherine evidently felt a deep obligation to support and encourage them, by her affection, her good humor, and her sharing of news, when visits were not possible.

By the time we get to December 7, 1840 – less than a year before her death – her letter to Sr. Mary de Sales White says "I know a few lines will be acceptable to you – a long letter is a formidable concern for me…perhaps I have told you this already…I must now keep a memorandum book to mark where I wrote and what I said. My memory is beginning to puzzle me: (p. 326, letter #215)

And this: "when I wake in the morning, I ask myself where I am – and on the last two or three foundations, I could not recollect for some minutes…" (p. 339).

This last comment of hers could well describe many of us now as we experience our own diminishing energies and capacities! During these times, Catherine serves as a further inspiration by her acceptance and spirit and most of all her undiminishing care for the sisters in their ongoing dilemmas.

c. *Resources sufficient to sustain houses and ministries*

The traces of these concerns are subtle and constant, riding through the letters like an underlined refrain. I will not list them here, as so often it was clear that Catherine asked other sisters to attend to the distress they brought to her. In any case, many are masked in other concerns. Instead, I will close this section with this quote from a long letter to Frances Warde, which included diagrams of beds and closets and windows, reports on behaviours and illnesses of some of the sisters, and concerns for the living needs of the sisters themselves:

"Take care you do not let this nonsense be subject to any eye but your own. (*If she only knew how far and how long these letters would be read!*) We have a majority of Bishops, after all events…"

"Pray fervently to God to take all bitterness from me. I can scarcely think of what has been done to me without resentment. May God forgive me and make me humble before He calls me into his presence."

"I went into town – and forgot this letter. I am so confused – and never dressed so neat and nice as my Dear Darling Fanny used to dress her old Mother. I am this moment in a fuss – at being obliged to appear in Disorder." (p. 142-43)

For all her cheerful fun and humorous expressions, especially of painful difficulties, I was particularly moved in writing this short reflection of her life as we know it by her recurring anxiety and emotional pain, which she successfully carried in the earlier years of her life. It is in the later years, as I offer below, that we see her directly expressing what she can no longer control; i.e., the limitations that come to everyone through aging and dying. Catherine McAuley, "our Mother" – as she is often referred to – walks with us even in this realm, as we all eventually experience. Her humanity is her ever present, ever-companioning presence with us all.

E. Visible/Invisible Presence of the Holy

As I read through Catherine's 256 letters day after day after day for about four months before I began to write this reflection, a stream of connection began to grow in feeling her presence and guidance in a way I had never felt before. The original inspiration for this writing began, as I have said, while standing in Catherine's Room at Baggot Street on Mercy Day, 2017, with that laughter at seeing her small writing desk and thinking how she would have loved email! On reflection now, it was that small seed of her presence – her invisible presence which I have sensed in that room more than once – that inspired the last section of this reflection: "the Visible/Invisible Presence of the Holy."

The first and most impressive indication to me of the "Visible Presence of the Holy" to me was Catherine's own humility, which I find especially present in the following letter to Frances Warde dated September 27, 1839: on p. 205:

"Sister Agnew is a delightful addition – every day more pleasing and amiable…always recollected, never too solemn – no show of any kind – yet all that is valuable shows itself continually…had I met her as she now is – 10 or 12 years since – *I might have greatly benefitted indeed, and even now she teaches me by her example what genuine meekness and humility are. The adage "never too old to learn" is a great comfort to me…*" (p. 205)

In January, 1839, Catherine wrote in a short history of the early years of the Sisters of Mercy, saying "we have been deficient enough – and far, very far, from cooperating generously with God in our regard, but we will try to do better…will try to repair the past." (p. 173, Mary Sullivan quoting Catherine McAuley from Letter 110).

And this familiar verse, which she wrote to Sr. Mary Elizabeth Moore in Limerick:
"Don't let crosses vex or tease,
Try to meet all with peace and ease,
notice the faults of every day
but often in a playful way.
And when you seriously complain
let it be known – to give you pain –
Attend to one thing at a time –
you've fifteen hours from six to nine –(letter of December 9, p. 170)

In a letter to Sister Mary de Sales we have one of Catherine's most famous spiritual teachings: making a

"passage through this world
like the dance called "right and left"…
and

"we have one solid comfort amidst
this little tripping about…
our hearts can always be in the same place."(p.332)

There is also an undated draft of a "horarium" that was developed for the sisters though in placement, it is in the 1840's. At the end of her outline, Catherine sums up by saying:

"This one day is our whole life." You might suppose the daily and uninterrupted repetition of the duties were tiresome. It is not so. Religious life affords more lively solid lasting happiness than all the variety this world could give." (p.314)

As I wrote this quote, I wondered what it would call from each of us reading this if we were to ponder that evocative sentence; "This one day is our whole life." Such simplicity, the depth of every day, is a characteristic of Catherine's presence and teaching of all who knew her, especially those early women who joined their lives with her vision.

Perhaps the best summary of Catherine's daily lived-out faith is summarized is a few sentences by Mary Sullivan taken from *The Bermondsey Annals,* in Sullivan, *Catherine McAuley,* p.117:

"Repeatedly, as Clare Moore knew, she had taught novices at Baggot Street "the advantages of Mercy above Charity." Her words are these: "The Charity of God would not avail us, if His Mercy did not come to our assistance. Mercy is more than Charity – for it not only bestows benefits, but it receives and pardons *again and again* – even the ungrateful." In Bermondsey in 1839, Catherine McAuley evidently felt the pardon and assistance of God; in the strength of such mercy she gave herself wholeheartedly to the foundation that – as it turned out – she would never see again."

There are many quotes about Catherine's devotion, and they are very familiar to Sisters of Mercy everywhere, which is why I will offer no more of them here. Their very familiarity, and the frequency with which they are used, easily give them that repetitive glaze of the too-often heard. Rather, I would like to underline that these evidences of Catherine's genuine faith and devotion as expressed in the language of her time are *even more significant* to us now. In many areas of the world – as some of our communities diminish in numbers, ministries and energies, even while other areas continue to go forward with sisters under sixty, and new members, how could we *hear* Catherine? What if we could rewrite her words and sentiments in the phrases of our own time? For hers are no easy prayers; they arise from deep suffering and challenges to her very faith, as any reading of her biographies will attest. Rather, I offer here something we don't often emphasize: the tender signs of Catherine's diminishment: November 1840 – November 1841.

The Luminous Ordinary
of Diminishment

If there is any phrase that will repeat itself in me after the loving adventure I have had in writing this reflection on what is known of Catherine's life, it is this phrase I was given as I began to gather my own interaction with what we know of her life: "the Luminous Ordinary." Catherine's words – their ordinary concerns, their tender worries, their humor and the laughter it must have engendered – and how most of her time was spent in writing these hundreds of letters we are beyond privileged to have for our own reading. If there is any theme at all besides the founding necessities of the Sisters of Mercy, it is the deep importance of ordinary life and our tender attention to one another. In these times, that seems primary.

In the last year of Catherine's life the signs of her diminishing health were readily evident. As I read of them, I can see them in the sisters of my own Congregation; I see them in the communities with whom I work; indeed, I see them in myself and in my own age group. Yet – "The most striking feature of this period is Catherine's fidelity to her duty as she perceived it, of letter-writing to the 'foreign powers,' her playful term for the Superiors and other sisters in the foundations outside Dublin." (Sullivan, *Correspondance, 310)*

Catherine evidently felt a deep obligation to support and encourage them, by her affection, her good humor, and her sharing of news, when visits were not possible." (p.310, in <u>Letters</u>)

It is through Catherine's own words, however - as usual in letters - that we come face to face with the serious nature and rapid decline of her health during her final year. Much of it comes from overwork as well as aging, but phrases like the following signify a slowing:

"I find I have written this already," (p. 328) and

"The ceremony is over and I am as usual –tired of doing nothing."(p.329)

"when I wake in the morning, I ask myself where I am – and on the last two or three foundations, I could not recollect for some minutes."(p. 339)

"My fingers are very cold and stiff. Let me have a long letter when you have time."(p.352)

Mark Nepo, one of the simplest most profound spiritual writers of our time, wrote in his most recent book *Things That Join the Sea and Sky*, a sentence that I kept repeating to myself as summing up Catherine's view of the world: "I keep discovering that everyone is lovable, magnificent, and flawed." (p.131)

If "flawed" means a bit edgy, cranky or impatient, which I know from reading the whole of the letters that Catherine could also be, these "imperfections" dearly allow me to feel more resonant with her as my own emerge in senior years. So often in these later letters she stops herself from going further with such remarks, such as these:

"I have felt quite anxious to write to you and my dear Sr. M. Xavier – but my old cough has made me so nervous that I could not – nor cannot now write distinctly. You must read with patience."(p. 364)

"I really forget if I wrote to you…but I think I did not…" (p.377)

Around this time her cough appears in earnest, when she refers to "taking Mr. Time into account, and wearing a "warm flannel dress," concluding with "I am now going to hide from the Doctor."(p. 367), then later saying:

"My cough remains as constant as your sweet little Mother's did." (to Sr. Mary Teresa Purcell, March 30, 1841, p. 379)

Yet, as late as August, 1841, Catherine was joking about being "Father McAuley, conducting the annual retreat at Baggot Street." (p. 409)

Again, thanks to Mary Sullivan, we see overall the subtle change that came about when Catherine's diseased lung began to be primary:

Only in the last two weeks of her life, when Catherine McAuley was bedridden, was there any alteration of her ministry. Then the humility that had long characterized her self-perception took the form of relinquishing to others, with encouraging confidence in their abilities, some of her personal responsibilities as superior, and doing what she could, in the days that remained… (p.435)

And finally, Catherine's rejection of the diagnosis of one of Ireland's foremost physicians – Dr. William Stokes – a few weeks before her death, echoes her personal resistance to the medical establishment of her time:

"My Right Lung was 'diseased' – I have now less confidence than ever in the faculty, [of medicine] and you know my stock was small enough. I do not think my lung is affected. I am now dead to the poor children – not to read or speak – give out office, etc. If my lung is actually engaged – the progress will not be checked, and the fact of no debility – not half so much as I have had when my gums were enflamed – shews that it cannot be.

As we should carefully examine the motive of our actions, I here humbly confess that my chief motive – just now – to shew that one of the most distinguished among our medical professors may be mistaken – and that we should not immediately take up their opinions." (to Sr. M. Aloysius Scott, September 26 or 24, 1841.) p. 442-3.

Catherine was well known throughout her life for doctoring herself. We also have references to her annoyance at Sr. M. Clare Augustine Moore's art work, and of her working around the needs and moods of Mary de Pazzi Delaney. She frequently spoke of her weariness at constant traveling, as well as her playfulness in writing nonsense poems and humorous letters to novices. She took delights in the St. Patrick's Day parade of teetotalers, and in making jokes about the physical situations she found herself in while traveling.

It was on August 20, 1841 – and November 11, 1841 – the day of her death, that we have her written will and the codicil that confirmed it.

And so it is on the morning of Friday, November 12, 1841 that Sr. Mary Ursula Frayne announces to Sr. Mary Ann Doyle in Tullamore:

Dear Rev'd. Mother,

Our dear and much belov'd Rev'd Mother is gone to receive the rewards of her good works. She departed this life after receiving the last sacraments, between the hours of 7 and 8 yesterday evening. May Almighty God strengthen us all, and enable [us] to submit with calm resignation to this heavy affliction. The Office and High Mass for the repose of her soul will take place on Monday at 11 o'clock.

your affectionately attached
in J.C.
Sister Mary Ursula Frayne

Conclusion: Following the Heart's Unfolding Vision

Catherine McAuley followed the unfolding vision of her heart. Although in her correspondance we find prayerful references, they do not dominate her letters. We know from tradition, and from the letters of those early sisters, of her daily life of deep devotion and prayer. Indeed, kneeling on her actual pre-dieu in the room where she died in Baggot St., in front of a life-size crucifix given her by one of the Bishops of her time, it is easy to know the depth of her devotion, to imagine the hours she spent there in the vagaries and worries of care for her sisters, for that is what dominates her letters: that deep care and attention, wrapped like a gift in humor and tenderness.

I am especially moved by these lines from "the Spirit of the Institute":

Therefore, reason and well-ordered charity require that we should not neglect ourselves for the advantage of others, or for any consideration whatever. We should not relent or grow negligent in our own improvement." (p. 459-60)

So, in concluding this long reflection, I am wondering what she would say now, in these times. I wonder what she would say about our diminishing numbers and capacities, the loss of our buildings and ministries, of energies and public presence. In fact, all through the writing of this document I believe now that this question was buried deep in the underground of my magnetic pull into Catherine's life. And now, coming to conclude this lively exploration (for that's what it has been for me), I can only conclude that she is still smiling.

For decades now, those of us who belong to her in that special sisterhood have brought her spirit and presence to schools and hospitals, into the homes of the poor and the poorest of the poor in deprived countries; indeed, into the places where Mercy in all its manifestations was and is now needed. That work continues and will continue. And – some of us are closer to this than others – like all forms of Divine Energy, the way it manifests will also transform, as it has done through centuries. For some of us, that process has well begun – as it always begins – with diminishment and disintegration.

Those outward forms are never the whole story, or even the most important part of the story. Mercy inhabited us, and it will continue to inhabit the world in forms we might never know and definitely never see. That is not only our faith: it is our knowing, our experience, and the spirit of Catherine McAuley begs us to recognize and connect with that knowing as she did: with humor, simplicity and grace; indeed, living every one of our days in the great light of the ordinary realities of our days, loving one another attentively and affectionately, as she did. Let our living these days be – as it was for her – the Luminous Ordinary. All is God.

From Catherine – Mercy is simple. It's reaching out, staying in touch, supporting one another in both difficult and easy times, and –yes – it's building schools and hospitals and other services for the people, wherever we live. But when these are gone – as is happening for some – how are we relating to one another? How do we deepen community? As Catherine did. As Catherine did."

"It commenced with two: Mary Ann Doyle and myself."

I close with two images that for me express the simplicity of that spirit of Mercy as I have known and lived it since I was six years old. The first is a sculpture by an Australian sculptor, Meliesa Judge, of Catherine McAuley. In it I see Catherine's young spirit, dancing and laughing – and offering, all of which I believe she never lost, to her last breath. The second is a drawing of my own, which to me expresses the simple essence of Mercy. See for yourself.

THE OFFERING

Catherine McAuley
Foundress of the Sisters of Mercy
1778 - 1841

Printed in the United States
By Bookmasters